We can Only Put Out The Fire, Not Catch What Started it.

Alice Taylor

BookLeaf Publishing

Presentation by *BookLeaf Publishing*

Web: www.bookleafpub.com

E-mail: info@bookleafpub.com

ISBN: 9789395413091

First edition 2022

DEDICATION

My Grandma Ada who used to love writing poetry.

ACKNOWLEDGEMENT

To Vanya, a friend who pushed me to finish and kept giving me the honest truth. As well as editing this book.
To Jamie who first gave me the titular quote when I needed it most.

PREFACE

Writing has always been a way for me to work
through my feelings. Putting pen to paper is
easier than speaking out and expressing them; a
way to ensure that my voice can be heard (or
seen) through all the noise around us.
The following poems are based on events that
happened to me, my interests, my beliefs, or
things I want to change.
It is split into 3 parts. The first is the good,
which is primarily positive things, my interests,
or just about me in general.
Second is the green, things in the environment
that can change if people make an effort.
Finally, we have the ugly. This is the ugliness of
peoples actions and my thoughts of them.
Hopefully, you can find some joy and comfort
from these words. Maybe even courage.

The good: Who am I?

I don't know who I am; who really does
The secret would make the whole world abuzz
I like theatre, and film, and a good book
Sitting to relax in a reading nook

I like to holiday and try new food
Most of these things, this book will allude
Disney and mythological creatures
Not all in this book are my best features

Environment is a passion of mine
Our beautiful Earth is on the decline
I want to try my best to make a change
These are poems that with you I exchange

The last bit is the oh, not so pleasant
The past, the future, and the present
Everyone has their own good and their bad
Personal things that make you sad or mad

Without further ado, have fun with reading
I hope the intro wasn't too misleading

The good: My reading nook

Calmness, ripples, clear blue
Relaxation, jets, green hue
Ocean, river, sea, and lake
My piece of mind does it make

Jacuzzi, view, rising sun
Lots of work do I get done
Window sill to write a book
How I love my reading nook

My wandering thoughts on this or that
People disturb me; there's idle chat
Sometimes I'm glad, sometimes I'm not
Good or bad thoughts are now forgot

Good company can help the calm to spread
At times I wish they would leave instead
Leave me at peace with just my book
Oh, how I love my reading nook

The good: Where to next?

Thailand, Miami, Morocco, Spain
Are they places I would go again?
If I return to places, definitely yes
But for now, I go once I must confess

The reason for this, I want to see all places
To learn languages and then to meet new faces
Cultures are different and entirely new
Each country I go needs adding to my tattoo

A map of the world in which I colour in
Antarctica is where I'd like to begin
The expense however is just too great
This trip is one that will have to wait

New Zealand another, but not on my own
I'm not a fan of travelling alone
Holiday groups are a new thing to try
I'm off on a plane, so long and goodbye

The good: Why do I like it?

Music, lyrics, fancy lights
Costumes, dresses, men in tights
Learning lines, make up, and hair
it takes months just to prepare

I like to watch and to do
Lots of fun for me and you
Get involved and then sing along
That's what makes a panto strong

Pyrotechnics and obscure sound
Theatre's where it can all be found
Musicals, panto, also plays
Fun and laughter they all will raise

My list is large, I've been plenty
10, 15 probably 20
No preference I'll give it a go
Will go see almost any show

The good: Untidy doesn't mean unclean

My room's a mess, always has been
Ever since I was a young teen
It is messy and not dirty
It should change now I am 30

What's a wardrobe? Mine's on the floor
Boxes of books and clothes galore
If I put on and change my mind
I take it off and chuck behind

I work a lot and say no time
State of my room should be a crime
I tidy but it don't take long
Things are chucked where they don't belong

My room's a mess and I'm not proud
I know it should not be allowed
Will do my best and try to clean
A clear room will now be seen

The good: All different

I've always loved the stories of Greek gods
Powerful beings defying all odds
The myths, the legends, the creatures the most
Magic and healing are powers they boast

The chimera's the one with many names
The dragon, whose breath is made up of flames
A cyclops, a giant with just one eye
A harpy, a woman with wings to fly

Hades, Poseidon, and Zeus, the big three
Poseidon's my favourite he leads the sea
Hades the Underworld and Zeus the sky
Fascinating stories I cannot deny

Look them up yourself I'm sure you'll agree
Although it's not something I'll guarantee
I surely love them and always have
In history they were always my fav.

The good: My mum's wedding

It's been a long time coming
More than ten years
Prosecco wine and many beers

The good and the bad
They have had it all
Sometimes driven up the wall

Both will deny it
But both have their habits
Doors ajar, research, and Abbot

Maybe not Abbot
But Drambuie or Stella
She couldn't find a nicer fella

Along with the doors
We can't forget snoring
Life with them will never be boring

Holidays galore like
Prague, Portugal, and cruises
In this marriage, no one loses

3 beautiful daughters and
a handsome son
2 grandkids, and many to come

He's been there for me
As much as he has her
A brilliant stepdad I definitely concur

I love them both
And wish them the best
Marriage to some is the ultimate test

Congrats to you both
And good luck to you too
Have fun and always stay true

No worries I'm done
I need to go
Let the fun begin and the drinks flow

The good: The great bird of flame

I touched before on mythical creatures
My favourite one is who this features
Traditional colours of red and gold
This particular one dislikes the cold

Legends say there are other options too
An icy version of purple and blue
But initial thoughts when thinking are red
Reborn from the ashes and flames instead

Dependent on belief its tears can heal
Their total beauty is almost unreal
Powerful bird means a powerful name
Majestic Phoenix, the great bird of flame

The green: Making the choice

To learn is the start, the beginning
What we can do, how we can change
Where we can adapt, or build or adjust

What can I do? What part do I play?
Be inspired. What do you love?
What do you see and are disgusted by?

Small Things do matter,
One person can make a difference
•   It's your city, your country, your earth

Make the choice, change your life
Make a start, however small
Recycle, don't litter, clean up

The green: Go gently

I want to help, but where do I start
It's not enough to just have a big heart
What can I do to reduce my waste
Plastic-free is not easily embraced

Plastic bags and such will kill all fish
Clear the ocean, that's my wish
Plastic cutlery should not be in use
We can avoid it too on most produce

If you grow your own veg and make your bread
Buy it from markets or bakers instead
If bought from these places they often have none
Your plastic-free life has certainly begun

Napkins and wet wipes should be discouraged
too
A flannel for them and for plates use bamboo
Single-use plastic avoid at all cost
Only use what will be kept and be washed

Gently does it, one thing at a time
Slowly but surely, will be a long climb
Conserve and protect, that is the key
Everyone can help, why don't they see

The green: Make Earth more cool

All our fossil fuels should stay in the ground
Taking it out causes trouble abound
Extraction of the oil, and gas, and coal
On our beautiful Earth, it takes its toll

Making greenhouse gases we need to stop
It destroys the ocean, humans, and crop
The atmosphere is destroyed and heated
If drilling the Earth is not retreated

Renewable energies, where to go
Solar wind and wave energy should grow
One big step is the power of solar
It reduces costs and saves bears polar

Another good step is power of wind
A cheap way for fossil fuels to be binned
Finally the power of the wave
Little is known but researching could save

Here, have some ideas for things to change
As solar power doesn't look so strange
Public transport, cycle, walk, and carpool

All of these things will make our Earth more
cool

The green: The Global Ocean Treaty

The ocean is an enormous force
Mysterious, and complex of course
So much that we still have yet to see
But when you look it's full of debris

The ocean is the Earth's thermostat
Though greenhouse gases are killing that
It helps in climate regulation
Need to stop acidification

PH goes down we need to adjust
With oxygen our oceans feed us
Without its nutrients, we are lost
Needs to change and my fingers are crossed

Microplastics in every part
Cleaning our oceans needs to now start
Killing all animals and our fish
Same creatures on your plate and your dish

Overfishing's one thing that must stop
Offshore drilling another to drop
Should try to eat less meaty
All sign the Global Ocean Treaty

The ugly: She said, I said

They don't like you, she said
It's just sympathy, she said
Words have meaning
Beliefs settle in
You worry it's true.

No friends, she said
Just mine, she said
She knows where to hit you
She knows what hurts
You start to believe

It may be true, to myself I said
Can't change the past, to myself I said
Truth or lie, fact or fiction
What she says doesn't matter
Your future is now

The ugly: I'm fine

It's not as easy as you may think
Just scream and fight, someone will come
I'm fine

Just run or hit back
I don't see a problem
I'm fine

I couldn't do it, I froze
I pushed, they pushed
I'm fine

Overpowered, they're stronger
I felt so weak
I'm fine

Naivety, inexperience, fear
Stop, didn't matter
I'm fine

Nightmares, androphobia, weight gain
Therapy, medication, diets
I'm not fine

The ugly: It's not my fault

It's not my fault
Don't blame me
I never asked
Why can't you see

I worked and worked
And it paid off
I did it myself
Now just buzz off

The stress is real
The job is hard
Feelings are felt
Don't disregard

Sure, money is good
It definitely has perks
But there's also cons
And customers are jerks

Not all the time
There's good ones too
We get loads of holiday
Let's go to Peru

The ugly: The tutor

She was not subtle, others noticed too
I always felt I was under review
Their opinions of me were then confused
For no reason were my feelings then bruised

They didn't know why the dislike was there
Assumed she was right to my own despair
It took them a while to see she was wrong
They saw it was her problem all along

People in power's opinions matter
Albeit wrong or right, does not matter
Criticism happened no matter what
Can guarantee I was always forgot

Did not matter how much work I put in
Was treated like some sort of evil jinn
Bullying was obvious and caused me hell
Counselling happened, she made me unwell

I ended the time with marks that weren't earned
They could not care less where they were
concerned
Marks got me forward but should have been
more

They rarely gave me a high enough score

I'm glad it's done, but gladder it's over
They certainly weren't my four-leaf clover
Won't see them again, my relief is real
So glad that with her I no longer deal

The ugly: Goodbye dear grandad

I won't say I'm glad to see you
Because the situation is bad
A funeral is nothing but sad.

Whilst the event isn't great
We're here for grandad Bailey
He will be missed, most definitely, daily

He was loved by all
No secrets to be had
A doting husband and loving dad

Cobblers were his team
The ones he did support
He spent lots of time on the bowls court

You may not know
But he liked to ice skate
He did it a lot with his lifemate

He worked most of his life
With a hammer and a lathe
A good meal did he always crave

His favourite by choice
Was a really good steak
and breakfast in which he would always partake

In the greenhouse
he spent a lot of his time
The fruit and veg were always sublime

Goodbye grandad here's where you leave,
We love you so much and now we will grieve

Perseverance is the key

Obviously, everything's not been easy
At times my life has made me feel queasy
Perseverance has definitely paid off
Even if people did laugh and did scoff

I've worked on well-being and mental health
Have tried really hard to better myself
People may not see just how hard I've tried
At times it's felt like I'm dying inside

But I carried on, I'm now much better
Writing it down like in one big letter
Maybe not letter but this book is here
Talking about things was my greatest fear

If you read and it helps well that's just great
It might just make you think and contemplate
It was hard enough to write it all down
So I'm sorry if it does make you frown

Some things within here I won't talk about
Don't bring it up if you're at all in doubt
Some feelings I have I'm happy to share
Just be considerate and aware

CPSIA information can be obtained
at www.ICGtesting.com
Printed in the USA
BVHW051948020623
665310BV00008B/99